SCHOOLKID'S CATHOLIC

BIBLE ACTIVITIES

ASCENSION

Time Period Name	Time Period Color	Book(s) of the Bible
Early World	Turquoise	Genesis 1–11
Patriarchs	Burgundy	Genesis 12–50
Egypt & Exodus	Red	Exodus
Desert Wanderings	Tan	Numbers
Conquest & Judges	Green	Joshua; Judges; 1 Samuel 1–8
Royal Kingdom	Purple	1 Samuel 9–31; 2 Samuel; 1 Kings 1–11
Divided Kingdom	Black	1 Kings 12–22; 2 Kings 1–16
Exile	Baby Blue	2 Kings 17–25
Return	Yellow	Ezra; Nehemiah
Maccabean Revolt	Orange	1 Maccabees
Messianic Fulfillment	Gold	Luke
The Church	White	Acts

All *Great Adventure Kids* books are color-coded to show where each story fits in Bible history. This makes it easy to discover how the people and events of the Bible fit together to reveal the remarkable story of our Faith. For more information, visit **ascensionpress.com**.

Originally published as *School Kids Best Activity Bible*
by Scandinavia Publishing (Copenhagen).

This edition published 2020
by Ascension Publishing, LLC.
Editorial Review by Amy Welborn.

Drejervej 15, DK-2400 Copenhagen, NV, Denmark
E-mail: info@sph.as, www.sph.as
Designed by Scandinavia Publishing House
Illustrator: Fabiano Fiorin
Text: Andrew Newton
Activities, layout, and cover: Collaborate Agency
Activity Editor: Linda Vium

Ascension
PO Box 1990
West Chester, PA 19380
1-800-376-0520

ISBN 978-1-950784-26-4

CONTENTS

God Makes Everything

Genesis 1–3

In the very beginning, God made the world, and it was all very good. He made the earth and the sea, the sun and the stars, the plants and the animals, and last of all he made the first man and the first woman. Their names were Adam and Eve, and they lived together with God in the beautiful Garden of Eden.

God had only one rule for Adam and Eve, and that was to never eat the fruit from the Tree of the Knowledge of Good and Evil. He warned them that if they ate from that tree, they would die.

One day, a snake tricked Eve into eating some of the fruit, and she gave some to Adam and he ate it, too. They were ashamed because they had sinned and disobeyed God. Now they could no longer live in the Garden with God.

Find and Count

How many of each item can you find? Write your answers in the boxes.

Pink Flowers ☐ Flying Birds ☐ Butterflies ☐ Horses ☐

Draw and Color

Design your own Garden of Eden.

Crossword

Fill in the blanks, using the story text to help you.

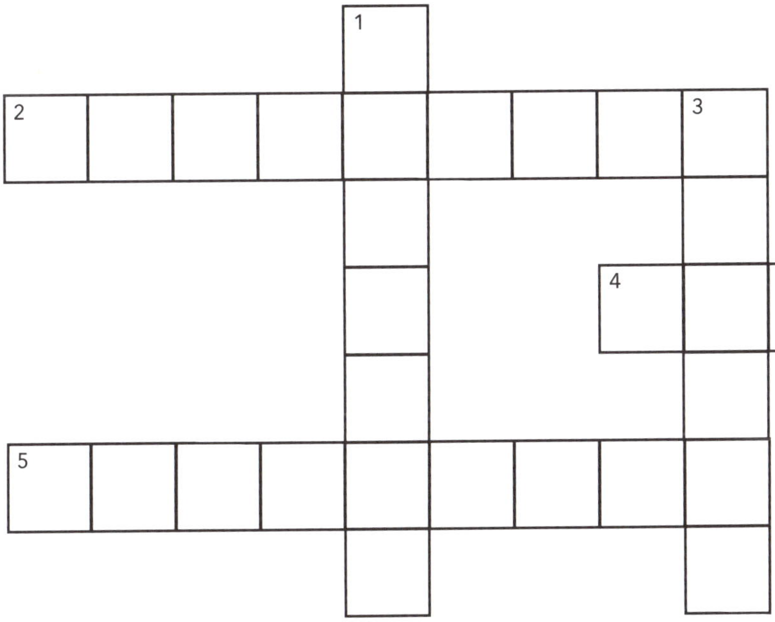

Across
2. The start of something
4. The making of something
5. Understanding

Down
1. Creatures
3. The ______ of Eden

Spot the Odd One

Find the odd one out in each row of pictures.

Descriptions

What part of God's universe is being described?

....

is the place that is made of water, where all the fish and sea creatures live.

....

is the place where the sun, moon, stars, and clouds are, and where the birds fly.

....

is the place where Adam and Eve walked, where the trees and flowers grow.

Color the Bible Verse

I praise you, for I am wondrously made.

Psalm 139:14

Dot to Dot

Connect the dots to see what is hiding in the Garden of Eden.

Noah Builds a Boat

Genesis 6–8

Because of sin, the world got worse and worse. One day, God saw that there was only one man who still loved him, and his name was Noah. God told Noah to build an ark, a big boat, because God was going to flood the world and destroy all the evil people. He sent two of every kind of animal to Noah to keep them safe from the flood in the ark.

Noah did what God told him. When Noah's family and the animals were all in the ark, God sent the flood. It rained and rained until the tallest mountains were covered. Noah and his family and the animals stayed in the ark until all the water had dried up again.

When Noah came out of the ark, he thanked God for protecting his family. God put a rainbow in the sky after forty days of rain and flooding, as a promise that he would never flood the whole earth again.

Sticker Game

Find the stickers on page 114 that complete the picture.

Color the Bible Verse

Fear not, for I am with you.

Isaiah 43:5

Maze

Find the route that takes you to the ark.

Spot the Differences

Can you find the 8 differences between these two pictures?

Descriptions

What animals are being described?

....

has a very long neck and is covered in a patchy pattern.

....

is a large black and white bear that eats shoots and leaves.

....

is a big gray animal with a trunk, tusks, and large flappy ears.

Word Scramble

Unscramble the animal names.

....

FRAGIFE

....

NADAP

....

LEPANTHE

....

DOCROLICE

Draw and Color

Color the rainbow and draw some animals under it.

Abraham and Sarah Trust God

Genesis 12:1–9, 21:1–7

There was a man named Abraham who loved God. He and his wife Sarah were both old, and they didn't have any children. God made a promise to Abraham that he would have as many descendants as there are stars in the sky, and all the people in the world would be blessed through him.

Abraham didn't know how God would do what he promised, but Abraham believed that God could and he would. One day, God told Abraham that in one year, Sarah would have a baby boy. Abraham and Sarah laughed because it seemed impossible, but God can do anything.

A year later, their son was born. They named him Isaac, which means "laughter," and they were filled with joy. God had kept his promise to give them a son, and he would keep his other promises as well.

Word Match

Draw a line between the words that mean the same thing.

PROMISE	**HAPPINESS**
BELIEVE	**DESCENDANTS**
LAUGHTER	**VOW**
CHILDREN	**TRUST**

Sequences

What image is missing from each sequence? Write the letter in the box.

1. 

2. 

A.  **B.**  **C.**  **D.** 

Shape Puzzle

Complete the scene with the shape stickers on page 115.

Dot to Dot

Connect the dots to see who is playing in the desert.

Key-Coded Coloring

Use the color key to color the picture.

▲ = purple ● = yellow ▼ = black ■ = brown

◆ = red ⬢ = blue ⬮ = orange

Family Tree

Each description is about someone from Abraham's family. Read each one carefully and write down the name of the person being described.

Abraham

Sarah

Isaac

....

the wife of Abraham and mother of Isaac.

....

whose name means "laughter."

....

would have as many descendants as there are stars in the sky.

Word Search

Find the words in the grid

B	T	B	L	E	J	X	C	U	A	J	R	P	S	F	T	A
A	F	V	E	Q	H	O	W	I	S	B	U	Q	D	O	N	U
U	D	L	M	U	K	R	Z	S	N	N	R	L	K	S	M	B
D	W	H	A	O	T	V	E	A	Y	F	P	A	I	A	Q	C
W	F	Z	R	U	E	R	Q	A	V	A	N	M	H	B	J	R
P	N	P	Q	H	G	K	O	C	Y	U	B	C	P	A	N	X
O	E	X	B	P	A	H	C	Y	K	T	D	T	G	L	M	V
I	S	A	R	A	H	J	T	R	V	X	Q	G	I	H	H	O
U	L	T	W	I	F	D	R	E	Y	J	Q	S	O	A	V	T
P	H	C	U	E	L	X	Z	M	R	F	E	L	W	M	R	Z

Abraham

Sarah

Isaac

Laughter

Joseph Saves His Family

Genesis 37, 39–45

Joseph had eleven brothers, but his father loved him the most. He even made Joseph a special coat. His brothers were jealous of Joseph, so they sold him as a slave in Egypt. God was watching over Joseph, though. One day the king of Egypt had a dream, and no one could tell him what it meant. One of the king's servants knew that God told Joseph the meanings of dreams, so the king told Joseph his dream.

Joseph told the king that his dream meant there would be seven years of plenty, followed by seven years of famine. The king put Joseph in charge of saving up food to prepare for the famine, making him the second most powerful person in Egypt.

When Joseph's family came to Egypt to buy food, he forgave them. "You meant to hurt me," he said, "but God used it for good, to save all your lives and many more."

Code Breaker

Fill in the Bible verse using the secret code.

A=1
B=2
C=3
D=4
E=5
F=6
G=7
H=8
I=9
J=10
K=11
L=12
M=13
N=14
O=15
P=16
Q=17
R=18
S=19
T=20
U=21
V=22
W=23
X=24
Y=25
Z=26

12 15 15 11 ◯◯◯◯, 9 ◯

16 21 20 ◯◯◯ 25 15 21 ◯◯◯ 9 14 ◯◯

3 8 1 18 7 5 ◯◯◯◯◯◯ 15 6 ◯◯

20 8 5 ◯◯◯ 23 8 15 12 5 ◯◯◯◯◯

12 1 14 4 ◯◯◯◯ 15 6 ◯◯

5 7 25 16 20 ◯◯◯◯◯.

Genesis 41:41 (NAB)

Crossword

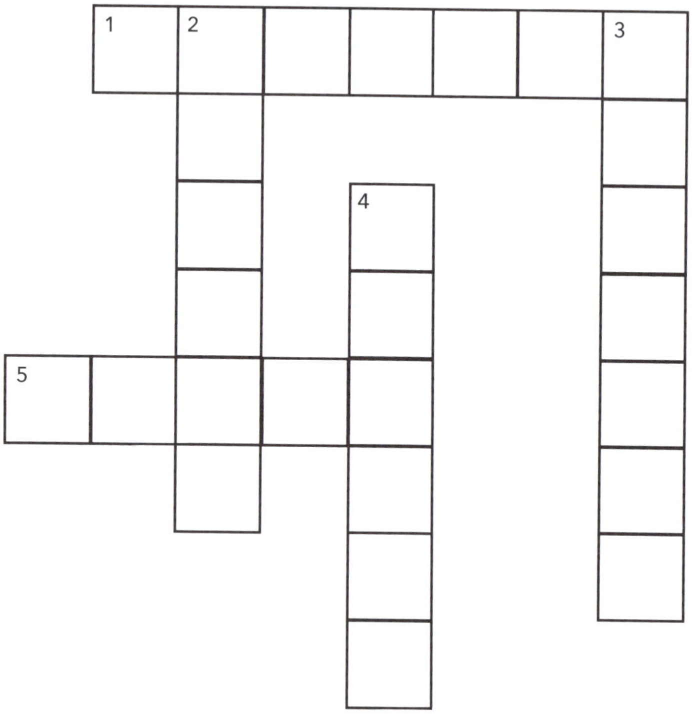

Use the story text to help you.

Across

1. How you feel when you want what somebody else has

5. A vision that comes in sleep

Down

2. One more than ten

3. A person in the service of another

4. A shortage of food

Story Quiz

Answer the questions about the story.

1. How many brothers did Joseph have?

2. Where was Joseph sold as a slave?

3. How many years of plenty were there?

4. Who had the dream that predicted the famine?

Draw and Color

Design a coat for Joseph.

Find and Count

How many of each item can you find? Write your answers in the boxes.

Palm Trees ☐ Sheep ☐ Walking Sticks ☐ Sandals ☐

Color the Bible Verse

For I know the plans I have for you.

Jeremiah 29:11

Line maze

Which line leads Joseph to his coat?

Moses Leads God's People to Freedom

Exodus 1–14

The king of Egypt was afraid of the Israelites, so he made them slaves and ordered that all their baby boys should be thrown into the Nile River. Moses' mother saved him by putting him in a floating basket. The king's daughter found him and raised him as her son.

When Moses was grown up, God appeared to him in a burning bush and told him to tell the king to let his people, the Israelites, go free. Moses did what God said, but the king refused to let God's people go. God sent ten plagues on Egypt until the king finally let the Israelites go.

After they left, the king changed his mind and chased them with an army, but God parted the sea so his people could escape. The king and his army tried to follow them, but God made the water go back over the king's army. God's people were safe!

Picture Sudoku

Every row and column needs one of each image. Write the letter of the missing image in each empty box.

A.  B.  C.  D. 

Maze

Follow the path through the sea.

Color the Bible Verse

Trust in the Lord with all your heart.

Proverbs 3:5

Puzzle

Where do the scrambled puzzle shapes go?

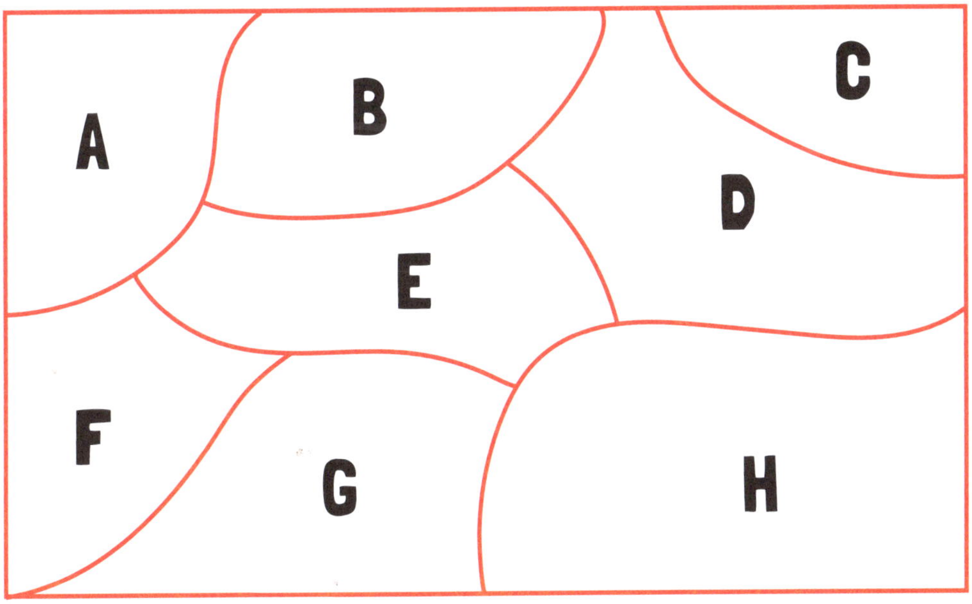

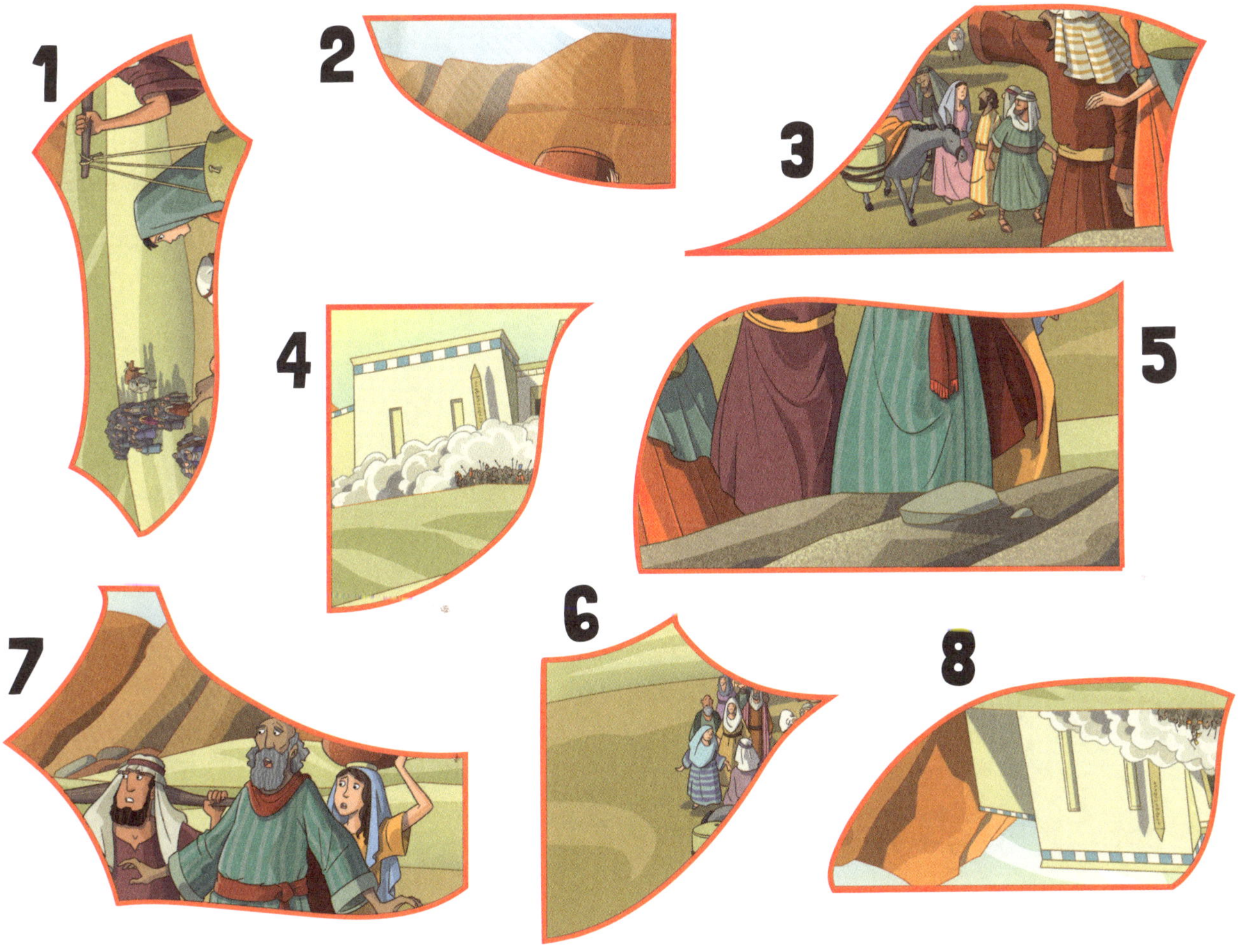

Spot the Differences

Can you find the 8 differences between these two pictures?

Spot the Odd One

In each row, find the picture that's different from the others.

Word Scramble

Unscramble the words from the story.

....

ELAIRSTIES

....

GAULPE

....

TYPEG

....

SEMOS

Ruth Stays with Naomi

The Book of Ruth

Naomi was living in the land of Moab with her husband and two sons. Unfortunately, Naomi's husband and sons died, leaving her and her daughters-in-law alone. Naomi decided to go back to Israel, and she told her daughters-in-law to find new husbands in Moab.

Her daughter-in-law Ruth refused. She said, "Where you go, I'll go, and where you stay, I'll stay." Ruth and Naomi came to Naomi's hometown of Bethlehem at harvest time, so Ruth went out in the fields to gather grain for them to eat.

The owner of the field Ruth went to was a relative of Naomi named Boaz. Boaz wanted to take care of Ruth and Naomi, so he gave Ruth as much grain as she could carry and told her to come back the next day. Later Boaz and Ruth got married and had a son. Naomi lived with them, happy to have a new family.

Spot the Differences

Can you find the 8 differences between these two pictures?

Code Breaker

Fill in the Bible verse using the secret code on page 23.

25 15 21 18   16 5 15 16 12 5   19 8 1 12 12

2 5   13 25   16 5 15 16 12 5,   1 14 4

25 15 21 18   7 15 4   13 25   7 15 4.

Ruth 1:16

Family Tree

Each description is about someone from Ruth's family. Read each one carefully and write down the name of the person being described.

.... *was related to Naomi and married Ruth.*

.... *was Ruth's mother-in-law. She returned to Bethlehem when her husband and sons died.*

.... *was Naomi's daughter-in-law and the wife of Boaz, who she had a son with.*

Key-Coded Coloring

Use the color key to color the picture.

▲ = red ● = orange ▼ = green ■ = brown ◆ = skin Color ⬢ = yellow

Find the Shadow

Which shadow matches the picture?

B.

A.

C.

Color the Bible Verse

Ask, and it will be given you; seek, and you will find.

Matthew 7:7

Shape Puzzle

Complete the scene with the shape stickers on page 115.

A Whale Swallows Jonah

The Book of Jonah

God told Jonah to go preach to the city of Nineveh and tell them to turn from their evil ways. Jonah hated Nineveh and wanted the people there to be destroyed for their sins, so he ran away and got on a boat going as far from Nineveh as possible.

That night, a storm was almost sinking the boat. Jonah told the sailors that it was his fault since he was running away from God. "You have to throw me overboard," he said. "Then the storm will stop." The sailors did what Jonah said, and as soon as he hit the water, the storm stopped.

God sent a big whale to swallow Jonah, and he was stuck in the whale's belly for three days. On the third day, the whale spit Jonah out on the shore, and this time he went straight to Nineveh. The Ninevites listened to Jonah's message and turned to God.

Line Maze

Which line takes Jonah to the whale?

Find the Shadow

Which shadow matches the picture?

Spot the Differences

Can you find the 8 differences between these two pictures?

Crossword

Use the story text to help you.

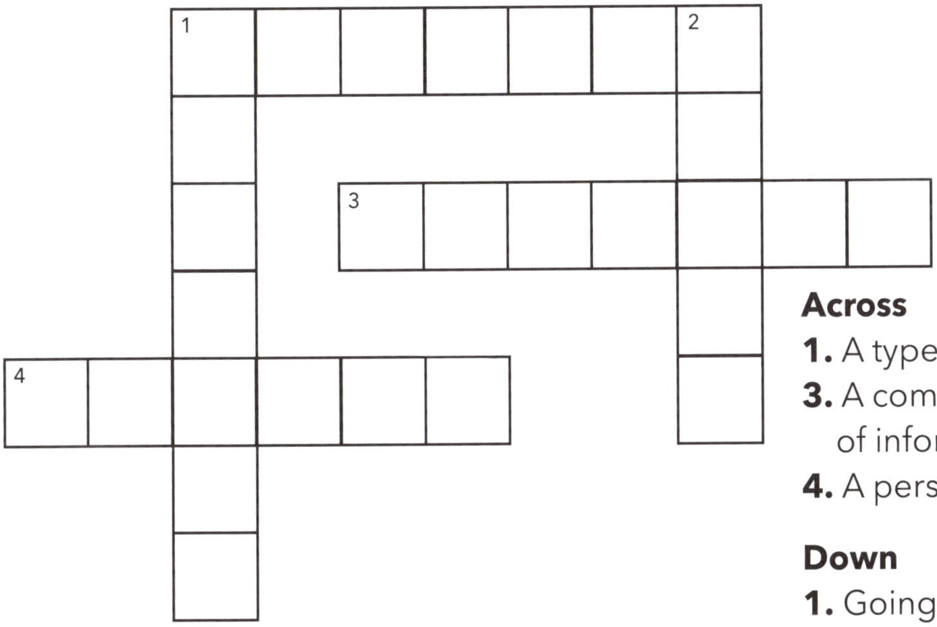

Across

1. A type of bird, or a gulp

3. A communicated piece of information

4. A person who sails

Down

1. Going down

2. A large animal that lives in the sea

Word Search

Find the words in the grid.

D	N	H	E	Y	R	A	K	P	B	V	U	C	N	V	T	Q
C	J	N	O	I	N	B	G	V	E	R	O	B	I	A	E	K
H	W	P	T	V	J	W	D	W	H	A	L	E	N	Z	X	W
E	Q	R	G	C	E	A	X	Y	U	M	E	Q	E	A	F	M
E	C	E	D	V	P	R	A	L	E	S	J	T	V	P	C	H
S	I	A	H	F	A	K	B	W	K	Z	N	D	I	D	C	G
M	X	C	P	O	R	B	J	O	P	E	P	R	T	W	G	H
B	L	H	Z	Q	I	Z	M	K	A	O	L	N	E	U	Y	R
V	J	O	N	A	H	B	F	X	W	R	C	U	S	P	L	J
T	S	E	S	Y	O	F	M	J	V	X	D	M	W	I	O	Z

Jonah

Ninevites

Overboard

Whale

Preach

Story Quiz

Answer the questions about the story.

1. Where did God tell Jonah to go?

....

2. Did Jonah like Nineveh?

....

3. Why did God send a storm?

....

4. What did the sailors do to stop the storm?

....

5. What happened when Jonah hit the water?

....

6. How long was Jonah stuck in the whale's belly?

....

7. How did Jonah escape the whale?

....

8. What happened when Jonah went to Nineveh?

....

Color the Bible Verse

The LORD is good to all, and his compassion is over all that he has made.

Psalm 145:9

God Protects Daniel

Daniel 6

Daniel lived in Babylon because God's people had been captured by the Babylonian kings. He loved God and was one of King Darius' most trusted advisers. The other advisers were jealous of Daniel, so they came up with a plan to get rid of him.

They went to Darius and said, "You should make a new law that everyone in the whole kingdom must pray to you and only to you. If anyone doesn't, that person must be thrown into the den of lions." Darius passed the law, but Daniel kept praying to God three times a day. The advisers told Darius that Daniel had broken the new law, and Darius was very sad. He had no choice but to throw Daniel into the lions' den.

The next day, Darius came to see if, somehow, Daniel was still alive. He was! God had protected Daniel and sent an angel to shut the lions' mouths.

Find and Count

How many lions are in the den?

Maze

Follow the path out of the lions' den.

Story Quiz

Answer the questions about the story.

1. Where did Daniel live?

....

2. How many times a day did Daniel pray?

....

3. What was the king's name?

....

4. What was the new law?

....

Puzzle

Where do the scrambled puzzle shapes go?

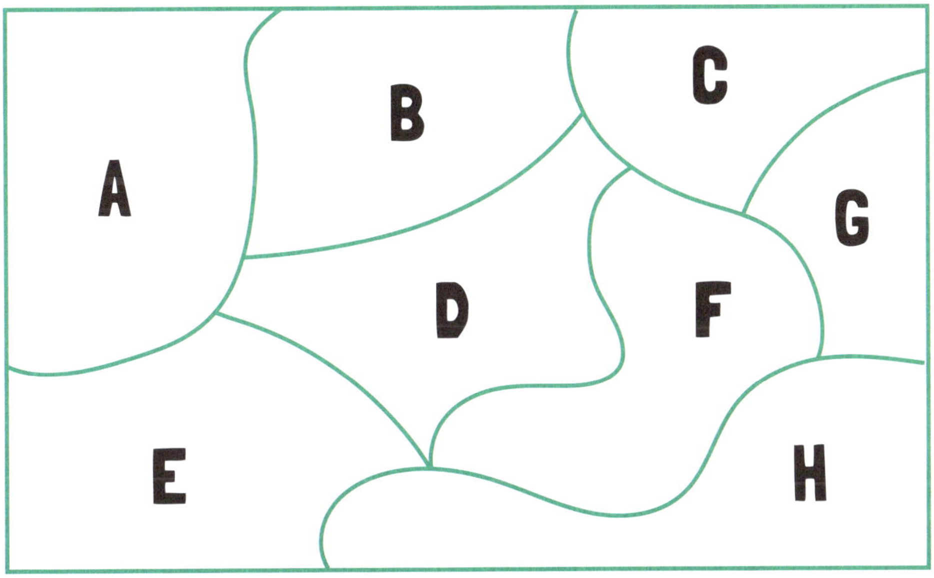

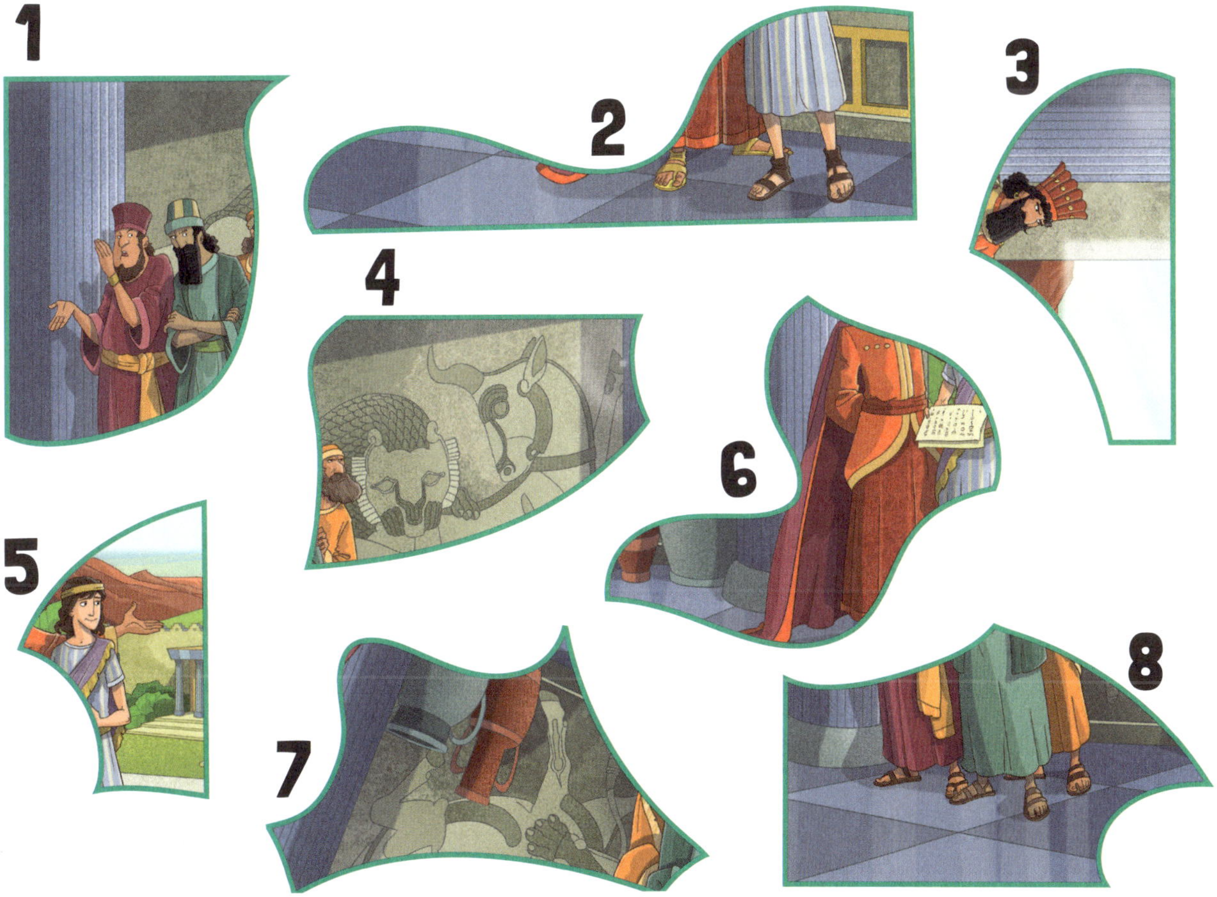

Descriptions

What elements from the story are being described? Fill in the blanks.

....

are big cats with sharp teeth and claws! The males have long manes.

....

is the place where Daniel was thrown for breaking the law.

....

was sent from God to shut the lions' mouths.

Word Scramble

Unscramble the words from the story.

....

LABOBYN

....

RIADSU

....

ELANDI

....

GRAPYIN

Picture Sudoku

Every row and column needs one of each image. Write the letter of the missing image in each empty box.

A.  B.  C.  D. 

Esther Saves Her People

The Book of Esther

Esther and her cousin Mordecai lived in the land of Persia, but they were Jews, God's Chosen People. Xerxes, the king of Persia, held a beauty contest to choose his new queen. He chose Esther out of all the young women in the kingdom to be his queen, but he didn't know she was a Jew.

Haman, one of Xerxes' advisers, hated Mordecai, so he asked the king to make a law ordering the death of all Jews. When Esther heard about this law, she went before the king, even though she hadn't been invited. She asked him to bring Haman to a dinner with her. When she was alone with Xerxes and Haman, Esther told the king all about Haman's plan to destroy her people. Xerxes was so angry that he had Haman executed the same way Haman had wanted to execute Mordecai. Then Mordecai and Esther made a new law that protected their people.

Word Search

Find the words in the grid.

N	R	Q	N	Z	M	K	B	W	R	W	E	P	J	A	Q	D
U	Z	E	M	G	A	I	N	D	Z	S	V	C	O	Z	V	O
Q	T	K	U	O	Y	N	J	U	J	E	S	T	H	E	R	H
H	X	V	C	E	R	A	O	X	G	M	X	Y	D	L	T	P
F	P	Y	V	S	A	D	Q	F	H	I	K	P	X	U	B	H
S	K	I	A	O	T	L	E	R	A	J	B	G	E	A	B	M
O	P	E	R	S	I	A	F	C	M	C	U	T	R	S	E	K
X	W	I	X	D	O	T	C	U	A	X	M	F	X	H	C	I
L	J	S	B	D	W	P	G	X	N	I	Z	K	E	C	N	R
H	E	Q	I	Y	L	V	M	F	G	R	W	Y	S	L	E	A

Mordecai

Esther

Xerxes

Persia

Haman

Word Scramble

Unscramble the words from the story.

CODEMIRA

SREXEX

ASPIRE

TEHSRE

Word Match

Draw a line between the words that mean the same thing.

COUSIN	PREFERRED
LAND	EMPIRE
CHOSEN	ALLURE
BEAUTY	COMPANION
KING	REGION
WOMAN	RULER
KINGDOM	KILL
ADVISER	RELATIVE
FRIEND	GUIDE
EXECUTE	FEMALE

Sequences

What image is missing from each sequence? Write the letter in the box.

1. 

2. 

A. 
B. 
C. 
D. 

Crossword

Use the story text to help you.

Across
2. Your aunt's son
4. Not welcome

Down
1. The main meal of the day
3. Attractiveness

Color the Bible Verse

Cast all your anxieties on him, for he cares about you.

1 Peter 5:7

Sticker Game

Find the stickers on page 114 to complete the picture.

The King Is Born

Matthew 2:1–12; Luke 2:1–20

Mary and her husband Joseph were traveling to Bethlehem, and she was very pregnant. This was not just any pregnancy, however. The baby she was carrying was Jesus, the Son of God. There was no room for them to stay in the inn, but the innkeeper had a stable where they could stay.

While they were there, Mary gave birth to her baby, Baby Jesus. Mary and Joseph were filled with joy to meet their baby who was God's own Son. Angels told nearby shepherds that the Savior of the world had been born, and they came to see him right away. A bright star shone down on the stable where Jesus was.

Far away, some wise men saw the star, and they traveled until they found Jesus. "We have come to worship the King of the Jews," they said, and they gave him gifts of gold, frankincense, and myrrh.

Dot to Dot

Connect the dots to see what animal is in the stable.

Spot the Odd One

Find the picture that's different from the others in each row.

Line Maze

Which line leads the wise man to his camel?

Sticker Game

Find the stickers on page 114 to complete the picture.

Maze

Follow the path to the manger.

Description

Match the gifts to their descriptions.

1. Gold

2. Frankincense

3. Myrrh

A. This gift is in a pot with a round lid. It is a rare spice that was reserved for the worship of God. This gift represents the fact that Jesus was indeed divine.

B. This gift is in a pot with a pointed lid. It is a rare spice that was used for burials. It is said to represent that Jesus came into the world to die for our sins.

C. This gift is in a rectangular box. It represents the fact that Jesus was royal and would rule the kingdom of God.

....

Word Scramble

Unscramble the words from the story.

....

ENINPREKE

....

HEDPRESH

....

SWIPROH

....

ROVSAI

Jesus Feeds a Huge Crowd

John 6:1–15

One day, a huge crowd of people had come to hear Jesus teach them about God's kingdom. There was no town nearby, and it was getting late, so they needed food. "You give them some food," Jesus told his disciples. The disciples looked around, but all they could find was a young boy with a packed lunch of two small fish and five small loaves of bread. Jesus told them to have everyone sit down.

There were more than five thousand people in the crowd, but Jesus thanked God for the food and started breaking it into pieces. He gave the pieces to the disciples to hand out to the crowd.

By the time they were done, everyone had enough to eat and was satisfied. They even had enough leftovers to fill twelve baskets! Everyone was amazed at the miracle Jesus had performed, and they said, "He must be the Prophet of God!"

Spot the Differences

Can you find the 8 differences between these two pictures?

Find and Count

How many of each item can you find in baskets 1 and 2?
Write your answers in the boxes.

Loaves of bread ☐ Fish heads ☑

Color the Bible Verse

Give thanks to the LORD, for he is good.

Psalm 107:1

Line Maze

Which line leads to the basket of fish?

Word Match

Draw a line between the words that mean the same thing.

HUNGRY	CONTENT
SATISFIED	ASTOUNDED
MIRACLE	RAVENOUS
AMAZED	PHENOMENON

Word Scramble

Unscramble the words from the story.

PLECSIDSI

IFHS

VOLASE

VRESLOTEF

Key-Coded Coloring

Use the color key to color the picture.

▲ = blue ● = brown ▼ = yellow ■ = red ◆ = green ⬢ = skin color

Jesus Welcomes the Little Children

Matthew 19:13–14

There were some parents who wanted to bring their children to see Jesus, but his disciples turned them away. "Jesus is too busy to be bothered with children," they said.

But Jesus corrected them. "Let the little children come to me," he said. "The kingdom of God belongs to children and people like them. In fact, if anyone comes to me and doesn't have faith like a small child, that person will not see the kingdom of heaven."

Jesus loves all people, young and old, big and small. He wants everyone to come to him.

Code Breaker

Fill in the Bible verse using the secret code on page 23.

23 8 15 5 22 5 18   18 5 3 5 9 22 5 19

20 8 9 19   3 8 9 12 4

9 14   13 25   14 1 13 5

18 5 3 5 9 22 5 19   13 5.

Luke 9:48

Find the Shadow

In each row, which shadow doesn't match the picture on the left?

Crossword

Use the story text to help you.

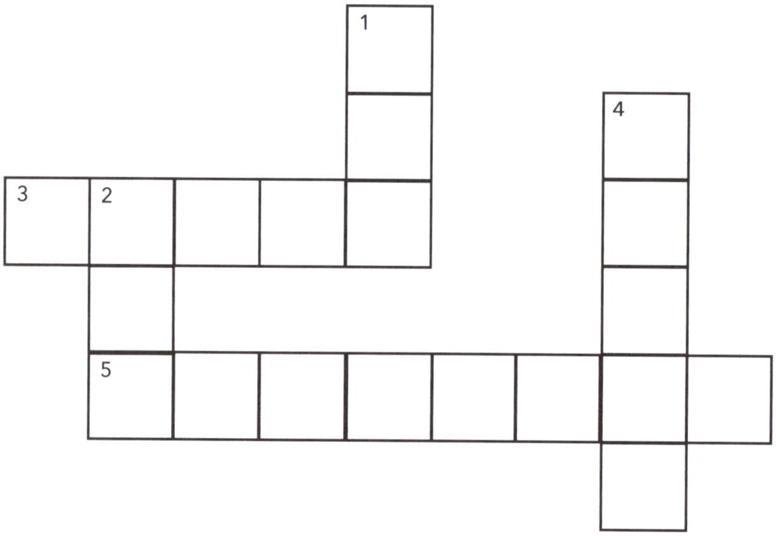

Across
3. Youthful, not very old
5. A follower of Jesus

Down
1. Alive for a long time
2. Large
4. Little

Word Search

Find the words in the grid.

D	Q	O	G	Z	S	E	T	Y	K	E	V	E	H	B	P	N
T	J	D	I	S	C	I	P	L	E	S	W	O	R	D	B	F
L	B	S	K	X	H	M	N	V	K	Z	H	L	A	H	J	K
W	N	F	A	Q	I	G	E	P	Q	I	H	M	I	C	U	T
C	O	I	Y	D	L	M	U	A	W	R	N	V	G	Q	Y	A
R	H	B	H	V	D	O	F	R	C	L	O	G	B	P	I	O
F	U	M	R	N	R	T	I	E	F	E	N	I	D	S	X	F
X	H	E	A	V	E	N	X	N	S	P	U	J	A	O	W	L
P	Q	L	O	D	N	M	Q	T	K	S	A	I	M	D	M	X
J	V	Z	B	S	P	Z	G	S	X	H	I	Q	C	Y	E	I

Parents
Disciples
Children
Kingdom
Heaven

Shape Puzzle

Complete the scene with the shape stickers on page 115.

Picture Sudoku

Every row and column needs one of each image.
Write the letter of the missing image in each empty box.

A.  **B.**  **C.**  **D.** 

Color the Bible Verse

Let the children come to me, and do not hinder them; for to such belongs the kingdom of God.

Luke 18:16

Zacchaeus Climbs a Tree

Luke 19:1–10

Zacchaeus was a very short man. He collected taxes for the government, and he often took more from people than he was supposed to and kept the extra for himself. When he heard that Jesus was in town, he wanted to see him. Since he was so short, Zacchaeus had to climb a tree to see over the crowd. When Jesus saw Zacchaeus up in the tree, he said, "Zacchaeus, come down from there. I want to come to your house today."

Zacchaeus was so excited! Jesus was coming to his house! He ran home and got a big feast ready for Jesus and his disciples. At the dinner, Zacchaeus said, "Teacher, I am going to give half of my belongings to the poor, and if I have cheated anyone, I will pay that person back four times as much!" Because Jesus showed his love to Zacchaeus, Zacchaeus wanted to show love to others, too.

Maze

Guide Zacchaeus to Jesus.

Color the Bible Verse

As far as the east is from the west, so far has he removed our sins from us.

Psalm 103:12 (NAB)

Spot the Differences

Can you find the 8 differences between these two pictures?

Puzzle

Where do the scrambled puzzle shapes go?

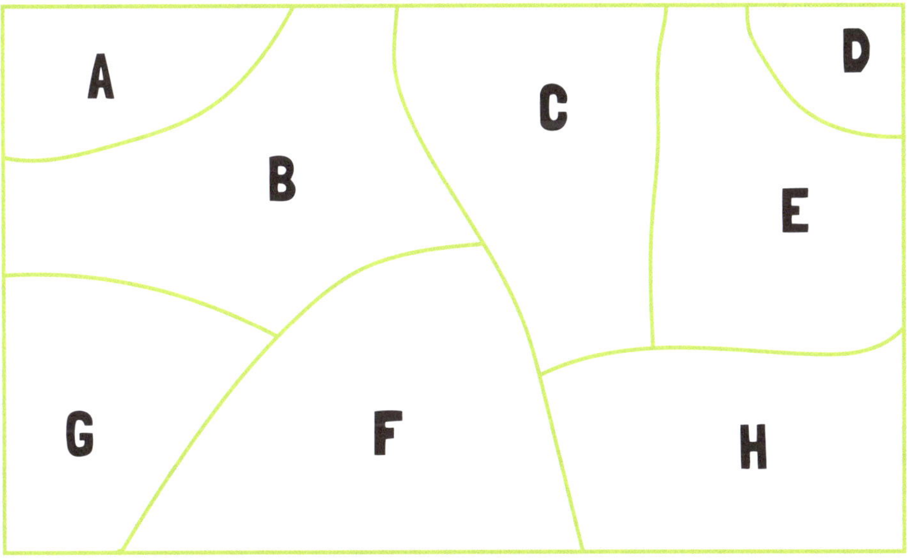

Dot to Dot

Connect the dots to see what the Roman guard is holding.

Crossword

Use the story text to help you.

Across

2. Acted unfairly

4. More than what's needed

5. A large plant with a trunk, branches, roots, and leaves

Down

1. Someone who instructs

3. Money citizens pay to the government

Sequences

What image is missing from each sequence? Write the letter in the box.

1. 

2. 

A.  **B.**  **C.**  **D.**  **E.** 

Jesus Dies for Our Sins

Matthew 27:11-66

Many religious leaders didn't like Jesus. They didn't understand his teaching. They were afraid because he was becoming popular. They thought that Jesus was doing something very wrong when he acted and spoke with God's authority and power. These religious leaders handed Jesus over to the Roman government. The Romans did not want trouble, so they agreed to crucify Jesus. This was the most painful way for someone to die. It was the way that the worst criminals were punished—but Jesus was perfect and had never sinned or done anything wrong.

Jesus was mocked. People asked him why, if he was so powerful, he couldn't save himself. Jesus carried his cross through the streets of Jerusalem. He was crucified between two thieves. His friend John and his mother Mary stayed by his side. When Jesus died on the Cross that Friday at three o'clock, darkness fell, and the earth shook.

Spot the Differences

Can you find the 8 differences between these two pictures?

Word Match

Draw a line between the words that mean the same thing.

LEADER	INTIMIDATE
THREATEN	LAWS
RULES	RULER
SUFFER	ENDURE

Word Scramble

Unscramble the words from the story.

TREPFEC

LRITA

NIULFAP

SEJUS

Story Quiz

Answer the questions about the story.

1. Why didn't the religious leaders like Jesus?

....

2. How was Jesus killed?

....

3. What did people say to mock Jesus?

....

4. Who stayed with Jesus at the Cross?

....

Word Search

Find the words in the grid.

J	W	F	L	Q	D	M	X	B	O	S	S	I	M	C	V	J
R	A	N	W	E	J	V	K	Q	M	E	I	P	N	W	H	A
D	P	O	T	T	N	C	V	R	H	Y	X	N	U	G	J	F
H	V	G	H	L	Y	S	H	P	W	N	V	I	F	R	P	D
U	F	O	R	G	I	V	E	N	E	S	S	O	H	U	T	G
I	T	J	E	B	U	G	Y	O	V	R	U	T	K	Q	L	T
B	M	I	A	L	K	C	R	U	C	I	F	I	X	I	O	N
K	P	N	T	H	N	A	W	J	U	M	F	E	W	M	I	P
R	F	X	E	W	L	G	D	H	B	N	E	P	C	S	A	C
C	Q	M	N	S	E	P	V	F	J	L	R	K	Y	T	X	E

Forgiveness
Crucifixion
Suffer
Threaten
Sinful
Perfect

Counting

How many crosses can you count? ☐

Sticker Game

Find the stickers on page 114 to complete the picture.

Jesus Rises Again

Matthew 28

After Jesus died, his disciples buried him in a tomb. Three days later, Mary Magdalene and another woman who also followed Jesus went to put some perfume on his body to keep it from smelling bad.

When they got to the tomb, the stone that blocked the entrance had been rolled away, and there were two angels sitting on it. The angels said, "Why are you looking for someone alive among the dead? Jesus isn't here. He has risen!"

The women ran back and told the disciples what the angels had said, and later Jesus even appeared to them in the house where they were staying. He let them touch him, and he ate with them. It was true! He was alive again! Jesus defeated death, and now anyone who believes in him will also rise again to live with him forever!

Crossword

Use the story text to help you.

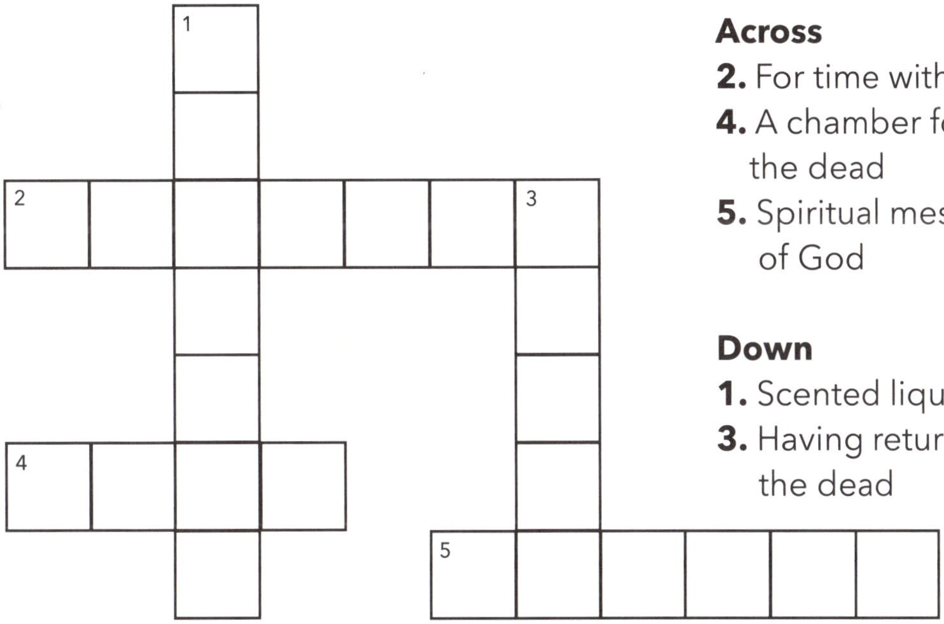

Across

2. For time without end

4. A chamber for burying the dead

5. Spiritual messengers of God

Down

1. Scented liquid

3. Having returned from the dead

Find the Shadow

Which shadow doesn't match the picture on the left?

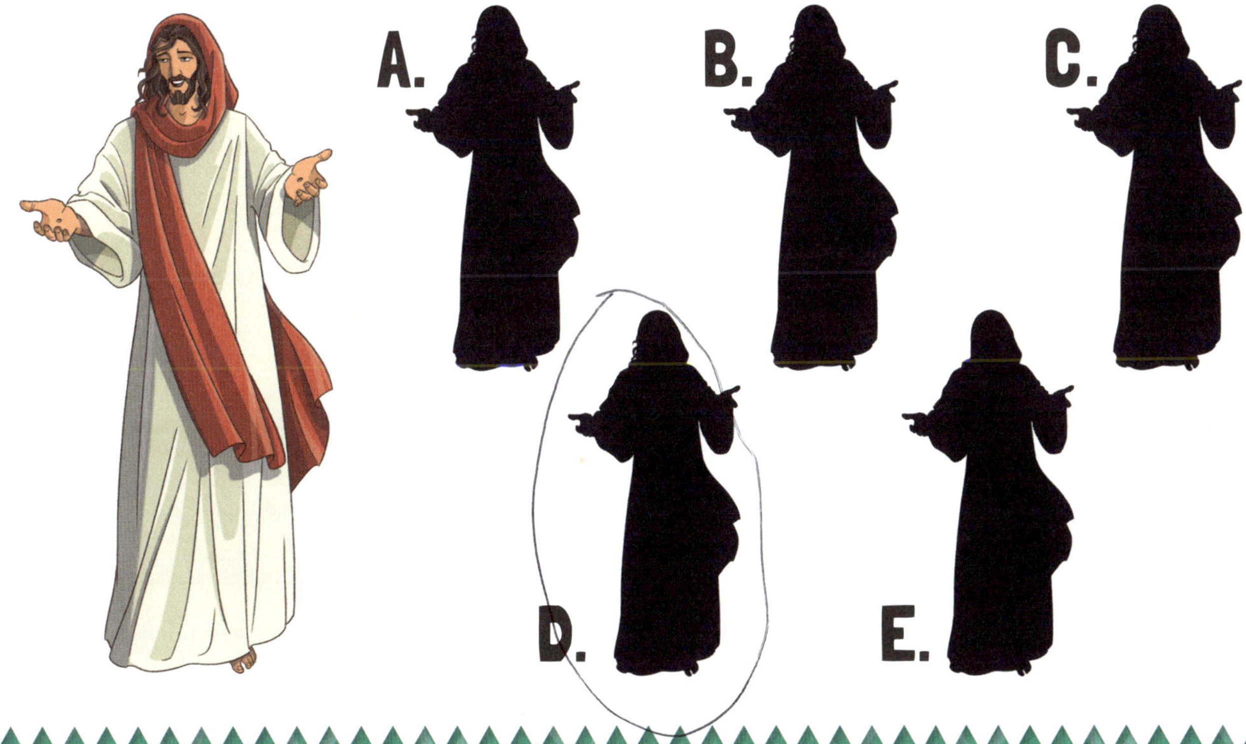

Shape Puzzle

Complete the scene with the shape stickers on page 115.

Color the Bible Verse

I am the resurrection and the life; whoever believes in me, even if he dies, will live.

John 11:25 (NAB)

Word Search

Find the words in the grid.

C	I	P	J	E	N	C	O	L	N	M	G	I	O	K	N	A
M	O	K	N	L	A	O	P	D	I	S	C	I	P	L	E	S
K	A	I	R	G	K	F	L	B	I	J	D	L	I	Q	L	H
F	W	G	Z	I	R	L	Q	I	H	R	N	P	M	J	A	J
O	O	G	D	P	E	R	F	U	M	E	N	A	K	L	N	I
B	M	D	G	A	I	O	K	J	P	N	L	N	I	E	Q	O
P	E	O	I	D	L	K	I	Q	D	A	K	G	F	P	B	M
H	N	M	L	J	K	E	L	O	N	G	P	E	J	L	M	C
K	E	J	I	M	B	R	N	R	I	O	R	L	P	C	K	R
A	P	L	F	J	I	H	Q	E	S	J	M	S	J	N	P	E

Angels
Magdalene
Perfume
Women
Disciples

Code Breaker

Fill in the Bible verse using the secret code on page 23.

9 ◯   1 ◯ 13 ◯   20 ◯ 8 ◯ 5 ◯

18 ◯ 5 ◯ 19 ◯ 21 ◯ 18 ◯ 18 ◯ 5 ◯ 3 ◯ 20 ◯ 9 ◯ 15 ◯ 14 ◯

1 ◯ 14 ◯ 4 ◯   20 ◯ 8 ◯ 5 ◯   12 ◯ 9 ◯ 6 ◯ 5 ◯ .

John 11:25

Maze

Follow the path to the tomb.

Saul Meets Jesus

Acts 9:1–19

Saul did not like the people who believed in Jesus and were telling others about him, so he got permission from the religious leaders to throw these Christians in prison. He even had some of them executed.

One day, when Saul was on his way to Damascus to arrest the Christians there, a bright light appeared in front of him. He fell off his horse and heard a voice say, "Saul, Saul, why are you persecuting me? I am Jesus, the One you are persecuting. Now, go to Damascus and a man named Ananias will tell you what to do."

When he got up, Saul was blind, so he had to have his companions lead him the rest of the way. Jesus told Ananias to help Saul, so Ananias went and prayed with Saul so he could see again. Saul changed his name to Paul, and he became a missionary, telling everyone he met about Jesus.

Find and Count

How many of each item can you find? Write your answers in the boxes.

Jars and pots ☐ Candles ☐ Windows ☐

Puzzle

Where do the scrambled puzzle shapes go?

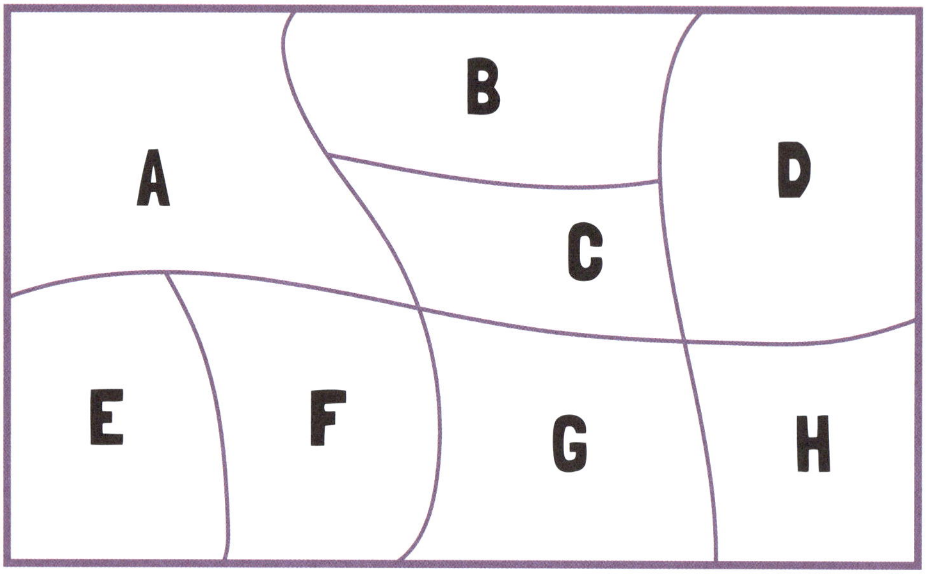

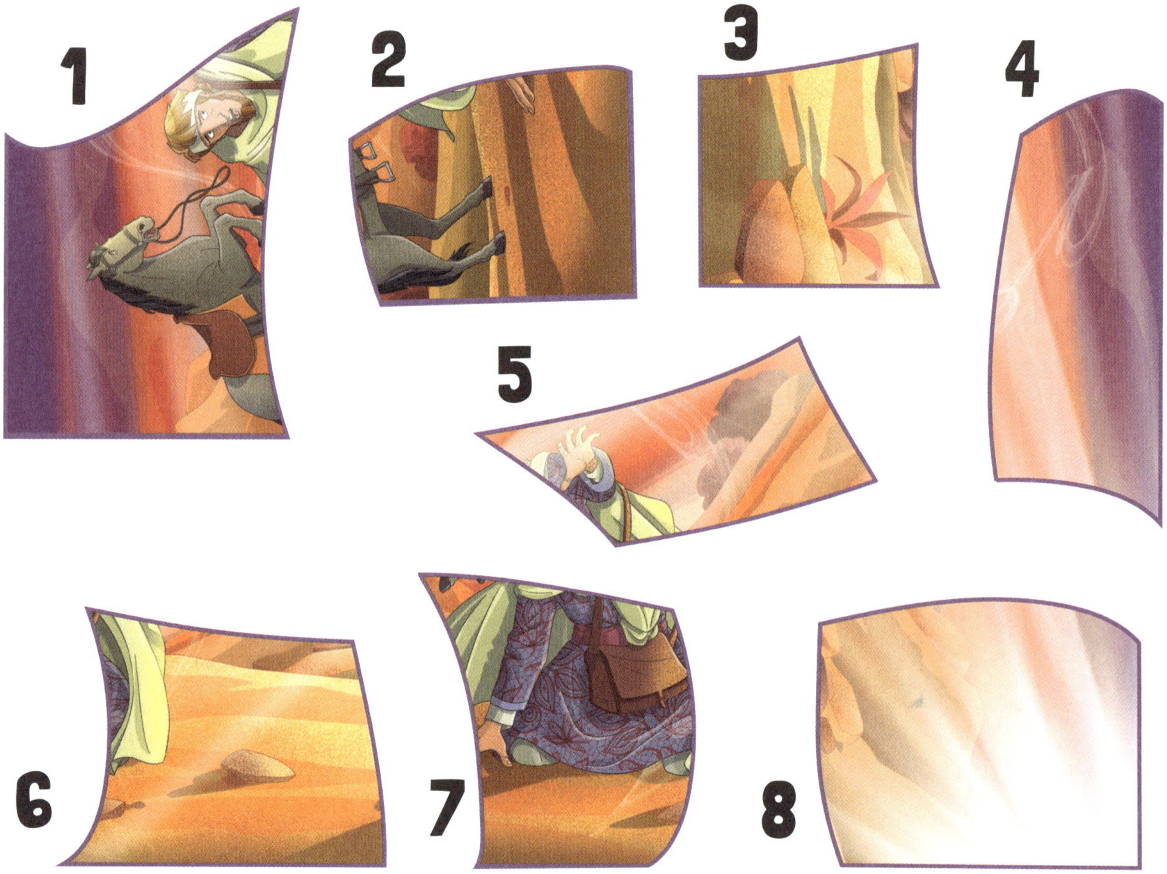

Sequences

What image is missing from each sequence? Write the letter in the box.

1. 

2. 

A.  B.  C.  D.  E. 

Color the Bible Verse

Everyone who
believes that
Jesus is the Christ
has been born of God.

1 John 5:1

Spot the Odd One

Find the picture in each row that's different from the others.

A.

B.

C.

D.

1.

2.

3.

4.

Find the Shadow

In each row, which shadow doesn't match the picture on the left?

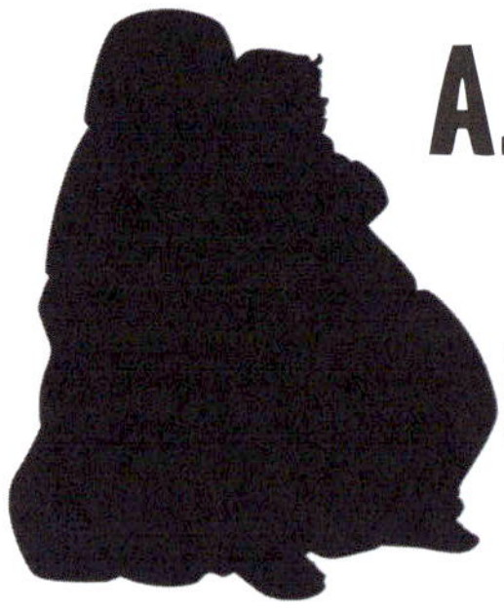

A.

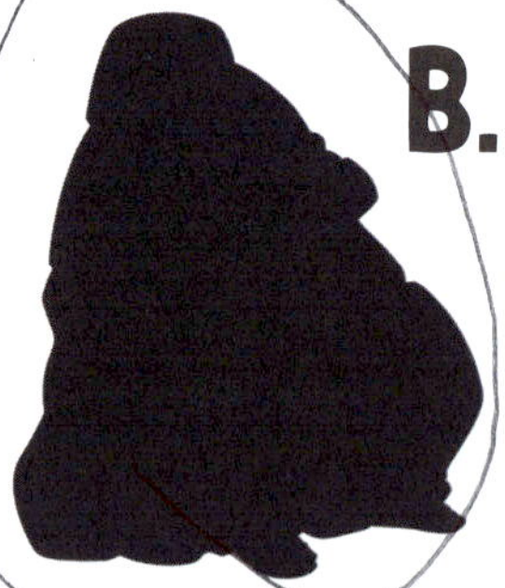

B.

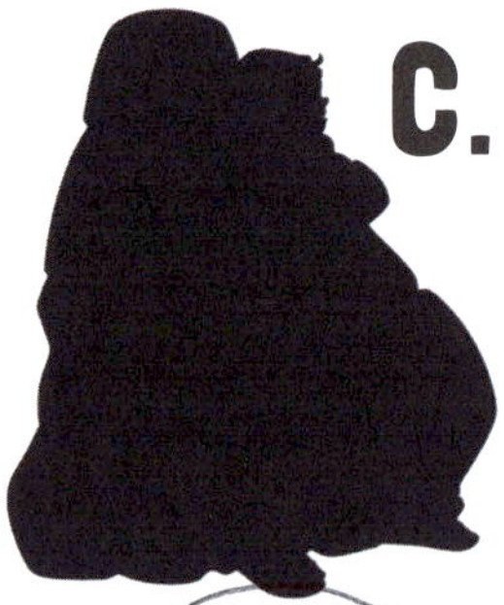

C.

1.

2.

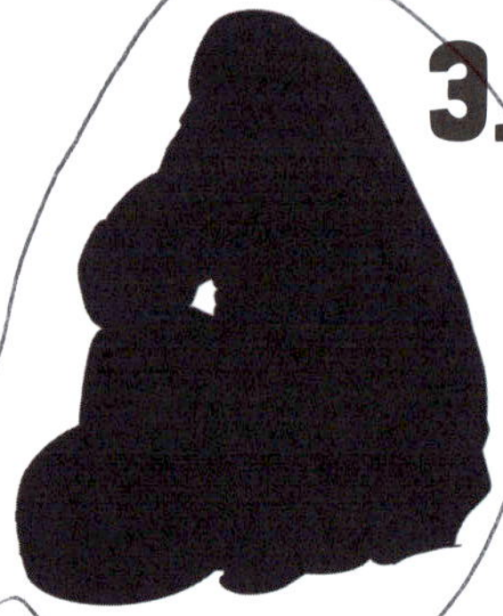

3.

Dot to Dot

Connect the dots to see what is in the desert with Paul.

Paul and Silas Praise God in Prison

Acts 16:16–34

Paul and his friend Silas were teaching people about Jesus when some important men in the town they were visiting got mad at them and threw them into prison. Paul and Silas didn't let that stop them from sharing the Good News about Jesus, though.

They sang songs and praised God right there in prison so the jailer and all the other prisoners could hear. About midnight, God sent an earthquake that shook the prison and opened all the doors and broke off all the chains. The jailer was afraid that all the prisoners had escaped and that he would be executed for letting them go. "Don't worry," Paul said. "We are all still here!"

The jailer asked Paul, "What do I need to do to be saved?"

"Believe in the Lord Jesus," Paul answered, "and you will be saved."

The jailer and his family believed in Jesus and were baptized that day.

Word Match

Draw a line between the words that mean the same thing.

TEACH	**KILL**
EXECUTE	**DESTROY**
BELIEF	**COACH**
BREAK	**FAITH**

Word Search

Find the words in the grid.

A	P	C	O	N	K	E	R	I	D	Y	N	B	X	J	I	G
J	M	T	H	A	S	V	M	W	Z	G	I	P	I	A	Y	Q
H	E	U	F	S	Q	J	U	P	A	U	L	C	K	E	U	E
J	R	J	Y	G	J	Q	A	T	R	H	U	L	W	J	B	E
I	O	W	E	A	L	P	R	I	S	O	N	E	R	Q	N	O
O	I	K	Z	S	G	J	Q	N	L	T	S	Q	S	P	S	H
M	D	M	C	X	U	Y	D	W	Z	E	V	G	I	Y	D	U
C	U	I	V	F	R	S	Z	G	A	M	R	T	L	G	X	M
R	L	T	A	Q	H	P	B	Y	B	Y	J	L	A	R	F	Q
E	O	F	S	I	D	O	A	E	X	K	H	Q	S	V	U	C

Paul

Silas

Jesus

Prisoner

Jailer

Code Breaker

Fill in the Bible verse using the secret code.

A=1
B=2
C=3
D=4
E=5
F=6
G=7
H=8
I=9
J=10
K=11
L=12
M=13
N=14
O=15
P=16
Q=17
R=18
S=19
T=20
U=21
V=22
W=23
X=24
Y=25
Z=26

18 5 10 15 9 3 5   9 14

○○○○○○○   ○○

20 8 5   12 15 18 4

○○○   ○○○○

1 12 23 1 25 19

○○○○○○.

Philippians 4:4

Spot the Differences

Can you find the 8 differences between these two pictures?

Sticker Game

Find the stickers on page 114 to complete the picture.

Crossword

Use the story text to help you.

Across

3. A shaking of the ground
4. Where criminals are locked up
5. Twelve o'clock at night

Down

1. Glorified
2. Rescued

Picture Sudoku

Every row and column needs one of each image.
Write the letter of the missing image in each empty box.

A. 

B. 

C. 

D. 

Game Solutions

Page 5

9 pink flowers, 10 flying birds, 13 butterflies, 6 horses

Page 7

Crossword

Across: 2. beginning, 4. creation, 5. knowledge.
Down: 1. animals, 3. Garden.

Spot the Odd One

6, B

Page 8

The sea, the sky, the land

Page 12

Page 13

Page 14

Descriptions

Giraffe, panda, elephant

Word Scramble

Giraffe, panda, elephant, crocodile

Page 17

Word Match

Promise = vow, believe = trust, laughter = happiness, children = descendants

Sequences

1. B, 2. D

Page 21

Family Tree

Sarah, Isaac, Abraham

Word Search

B	T	B	L	E	J	X	C	U	A	J	R	P	S	F	T	A
A	F	V	E	Q	H	O	W	I	S	B	U	Q	D	O	N	U
U	D	L	M	U	K	R	Z	S	N	N	R	L	K	S	M	B
D	W	H	A	O	T	V	E	A	Y	F	P	A	I	A	Q	C
W	F	Z	R	U	E	R	Q	A	V	A	N	M	H	B	J	R
P	N	P	Q	H	G	K	O	C	Y	U	B	C	P	A	N	X
O	E	X	B	P	A	H	C	Y	K	T	D	T	G	L	M	V
I	S	A	R	A	H	J	T	R	V	X	Q	G	I	H	H	O
U	L	T	W	I	F	D	R	E	Y	J	Q	S	O	A	V	T
P	H	C	U	E	L	X	Z	M	R	F	E	L	W	M	R	Z

Page 23

"Look, I put you in charge of the whole land of Egypt."

Page 24

Crossword

Across: 1. jealous, 5. dream.
Down: 2. eleven, 3. servant, 4. famine.

Story Quiz

1. eleven, 2. Egypt, 3. seven, 4. the king

Page 26

4 palm trees, 9 sheep, 2 walking sticks, 11 sandals

Game Solutions

Page 27
B

Page 29

Page 30

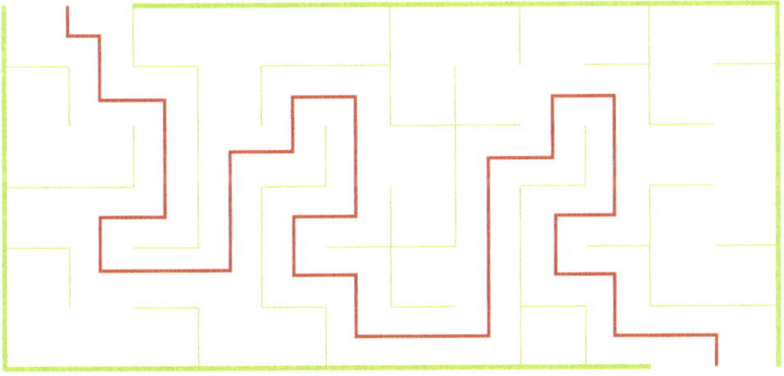

Page 31
A. 4, B. 8, C. 2, D. 7, E. 1, F. 6, G.3, H.5

Page 32

Page 33
Spot the Odd One
4, C

Word Scramble
Israelites, plague, Egypt, Moses

Page 35

Page 36
Code Breaker
"Your people shall be my people, and your God my God."

Family Tree
Boaz, Naomi, Ruth

Page 37
B

Page 41
Line Maze
A

Find the Shadow
C

Page 42

Page 43
Crossword
Across: 1. swallow, 3. message, 4. sailor. Down: 1. sinking, 2. whale.

Game Solutions

Word Search

D	N	H	E	Y	R	A	K	P	B	V	U	C	N	V	T	Q
C	J	N	O	I	N	B	G	V	E	R	O	B	I	A	E	K
H	W	P	T	V	J	W	D	W	H	A	L	E	N	Z	X	W
E	Q	R	G	C	E	A	X	Y	U	M	E	Q	E	A	F	M
E	C	E	D	V	P	R	A	L	E	S	J	T	V	P	C	H
S	I	A	H	F	A	K	B	W	K	Z	N	D	I	D	C	G
M	X	C	P	O	R	B	J	O	P	E	P	R	T	W	G	H
B	L	H	Z	Q	I	Z	M	K	A	O	L	N	E	U	Y	R
V	J	O	N	A	H	B	F	X	W	R	C	U	S	P	L	J
T	S	E	S	Y	O	F	M	J	V	X	D	M	W	I	O	Z

Page 44

1. Nineveh. 2. No. 3. Because Jonah was running away. 4. They threw Jonah overboard. 5. The storm stopped. 6. Three days. 7. The whale spat him out on the shore. 8. The Ninevites listened to Jonah's message and turned to God.

Page 47

18 lions

Page 48

Maze

Story Quiz

1. Babylon, 2. three, 3. Darius, 4. everyone in the kingdom must pray only to the king.

Page 49

A. 1, B. 4, C. 3, D. 7, E. 8, F. 6, G. 5, H. 2

Page 50

Descriptions

Lions, the lions' den, an angel

Word Scramble

Babylon, Darius, Daniel, praying

Page 51

Page 53

Word Search

N	R	Q	N	Z	M	K	B	W	R	W	E	P	J	A	Q	D
U	Z	E	M	G	A	I	N	D	Z	S	V	C	O	Z	V	O
Q	T	K	U	O	Y	N	J	U	J	E	S	T	H	E	R	H
H	X	V	C	E	R	A	O	X	G	M	X	Y	D	L	T	P
F	P	Y	V	S	A	D	Q	F	H	I	K	P	X	U	B	H
S	K	I	A	O	T	L	E	R	A	J	B	G	E	A	B	M
O	P	E	R	S	I	A	F	C	M	C	U	T	R	S	E	K
X	W	I	X	D	O	T	C	U	A	X	M	F	X	H	C	I
L	J	S	B	D	W	P	G	X	N	I	Z	K	E	C	N	R
H	E	Q	I	Y	L	V	M	F	G	R	W	Y	S	L	E	A

Word Scramble

Mordecai, Xerxes, Persia, Esther

Page 54

Cousin = relative, land = region, chosen = preferred, beauty = allure, king = ruler, woman = female, kingdom = empire, adviser = guide, friend = companion, execute = kill

Page 55

Sequences

1. B, 2.C

Crossword

Across: 2. cousin, 4. uninvited.
Down: 1. dinner, 3. beauty.

Game Solutions

Page 60

Spot the Odd One

4, B

Line Maze

A

Page 62

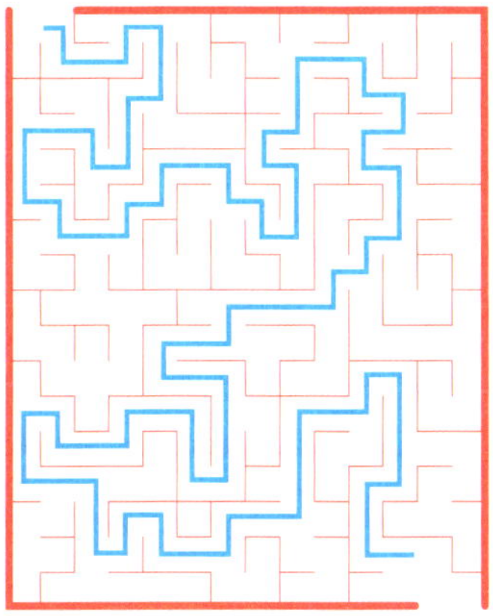

Page 63

Description

1. C, 2. A, 3. B

Word Scramble

Innkeeper, shepherd, worship, savior

Page 65

Page 66

4 loaves of bread, 2 fish heads

Page 67

C

Page 68

Word Match

Hungry = ravenous, satisfied = content, miracle = phenomenon, amazed = astounded

Word Scramble

Disciples, fish, loaves, leftovers

Page 71

Code Breaker

"Whoever receives this child in my name receives me."

Find the Shadow

4, A

Page 72

Crossword

Across: 3. young, 5. disciple.
Down: 1. old, 2. big, 4. small.

Word Search

D	Q	O	G	Z	S	E	T	Y	K	E	V	E	H	B	P	N
T	J	D	I	S	C	I	P	L	E	S	W	O	R	D	B	F
L	B	S	K	X	H	M	N	V	K	Z	H	L	A	H	J	K
W	N	F	A	Q	I	G	E	P	Q	I	H	M	I	C	U	T
C	O	I	Y	D	L	M	U	A	W	R	N	V	G	Q	Y	A
R	H	B	H	V	D	O	F	R	C	L	O	G	B	P	I	O
F	U	M	R	N	R	T	I	E	F	E	N	I	D	S	X	F
X	H	E	A	V	E	N	X	N	S	P	U	J	A	O	W	L
P	Q	L	O	D	N	M	Q	T	K	S	A	I	M	D	M	X
J	V	Z	B	S	P	Z	G	S	X	H	I	Q	C	Y	E	I

Page 74

Game Solutions

Page 77

Page 78

Page 79

A. 3, B. 2, C. 6, D. 5, E. 1, F. 8, G. 4, H. 7

Page 81

Crossword

Across: 2. cheated, 4. extra, 5. tree.
Down: 1. teacher, 3. taxes

Sequences

1. A, 2. C

Page 83

Page 84

Word Match

Leader = ruler, threaten = intimidate, rules = laws, suffer = endure

Word Scramble

Perfect, trial, painful, Jesus

Page 85

Story Quiz

1. They didn't understand his teaching. 2. He was crucified. 3. If you're so powerful, why can't you save yourself? 4. His friend John and his mother Mary.

Word Search

J	W	F	L	Q	D	M	X	B	O	S	S	I	M	C	V	J
R	A	N	W	E	J	V	K	Q	M	E	I	P	N	W	H	A
D	P	O	T	T	N	C	V	R	H	Y	X	N	U	G	J	F
H	V	G	H	L	Y	S	H	P	W	N	V	I	F	R	P	D
U	F	O	R	G	I	V	E	N	E	S	S	O	H	U	T	G
I	T	J	E	B	U	G	Y	O	V	R	U	T	K	Q	L	T
B	M	I	A	L	K	C	R	U	C	I	F	I	X	I	O	N
K	P	N	T	H	N	A	W	J	U	M	F	E	W	M	I	P
R	F	X	E	W	L	G	D	H	B	N	E	P	C	S	A	C
C	Q	M	N	S	E	P	V	F	J	L	R	K	Y	T	X	E

Page 86

33

Page 89

Crossword

Across: 2. forever, 4. tomb, 5. angels.
Down: 1. perfume, 3. risen.

Find the Shadow

E

Game Solutions

Page 92

Word Search

C	I	P	J	E	N	C	O	L	N	M	G	I	O	K	N	A
M	O	K	N	L	A	O	P	D	I	S	C	I	P	L	E	S
K	A	I	R	G	K	F	L	B	I	J	D	L	I	Q	L	H
F	W	G	Z	I	R	L	Q	I	H	R	N	P	M	J	A	J
O	O	G	D	P	E	R	F	U	M	E	N	A	K	L	N	I
B	M	D	G	A	I	O	K	J	P	N	L	N	I	E	Q	O
P	E	O	I	D	L	K	I	Q	D	A	K	G	F	P	B	M
H	N	M	L	J	K	E	L	O	N	G	P	E	J	L	M	C
K	E	J	I	M	B	R	N	R	I	O	R	L	P	C	K	R
A	P	L	F	J	I	H	Q	E	S	J	M	S	J	N	P	E

Code Breaker

"I am the resurrection and the life."

Page 93

Page 95

6 Jars and pots, 3 candles, 2 windows

Page 96

A. 1, B. 4, C. 5, D. 8, E. 2, F. 7, G. 6, H. 3

Page 97

1. B, 2.C

Page 98

Spot the Odd One

D, 2

Find the Shadow

B, 3

Page 101

Word Match

Teach = coach, execute = kill, belief = faith, break = destroy

Word Search

A	P	C	O	N	K	E	R	I	D	Y	N	B	X	J	I	G
J	M	T	H	A	S	V	M	W	Z	G	I	P	I	A	Y	Q
H	E	U	F	S	Q	J	U	P	A	U	L	C	K	E	U	E
J	R	J	Y	G	J	Q	A	T	R	H	U	L	W	J	B	E
I	O	W	E	A	L	P	R	I	S	O	N	E	R	Q	N	O
O	I	K	Z	S	G	J	Q	N	L	T	S	Q	S	P	S	H
M	D	M	C	X	U	Y	D	W	Z	E	V	G	I	Y	D	U
C	U	I	V	F	R	S	Z	G	A	M	R	T	L	G	X	M
R	L	T	A	Q	H	P	B	Y	B	Y	J	L	A	R	F	Q
E	O	F	S	I	D	O	A	E	X	K	H	Q	S	V	U	C

Page 102

"Rejoice in the Lord always."

Page 103

Page 105

Crossword

Across: 3. earthquake, 4. prison, 5. midnight. Down: 1. risen, 2. saved.

Picture Sudoku